THE MOON OF THE
SALAMANDERS

THE THIRTEEN MOONS

The Moon of the Owls (JANUARY)

The Moon of the Bears (FEBRUARY)

The Moon of the Salamanders (MARCH)

The Moon of the Chickarees (APRIL)

The Moon of the Monarch Butterflies (MAY)

The Moon of the Fox Pups (JUNE)

The Moon of the Wild Pigs (JULY)

The Moon of the Mountain Lions (AUGUST)

The Moon of the Deer (SEPTEMBER)

The Moon of the Alligators (OCTOBER)

The Moon of the Gray Wolves (NOVEMBER)

The Moon of the Winter Bird (DECEMBER)

The Moon of the Moles (DECEMBER–JANUARY)

NEW EDITION   THE THIRTEEN MOONS

THE MOON OF THE SALAMANDERS

BY JEAN CRAIGHEAD GEORGE

ILLUSTRATED BY MARLENE HILL WERNER

HarperCollins*Publishers*

The illustrations in this book were painted with
acrylic paints on watercolor board.

The Moon of the Salamanders
Text copyright © 1967, 1992 by Jean Craighead George
Illustrations copyright © 1992 by Marlene Hill Werner

Typography by Al Cetta
1   2   3   4   5   6   7   8   9   10
NEW EDITION

Library of Congress Cataloging-in-Publication Data
George, Jean Craighead, date
    The moon of the salamanders / by Jean Craighead George ;
illustrated by Marlene Hill Werner. — New ed.
        p.   cm. — (The Thirteen moons)
    Summary: On a rainy March night, a salamander returns to the
spring pond for the ancient mating dance of the salamanders.
    ISBN 0-06-022609-9. — ISBN 0-06-022694-3 (lib. bdg.)
    1. Salamanders—Juvenile literature.   2. Salamanders—
Michigan—Juvenile literature.   [1. Salamanders.]   I. Werner,
Marlene Hill, ill.   II. Title.   III. Series: George, Jean Craighead,
date, Thirteen moons (HarperCollins)
QL795.S3G4   1992   90-25591
597.6'5—dc20   CIP
                                                              AC

Why is this series called The Thirteen Moons?

Each year there are either thirteen full moons or thirteen new moons. This series of books is named in their honor.

Our culture, which bases its calendar on sun-time, has no names for the thirteen moons. I have named the thirteen lunar months after thirteen North American animals. Primarily night prowlers, these animals, at a particular time of the year in a particular place, do wondrous things. The places are known to you, but the animal moon names are not because I made them up. So that you can place them on our sun calendar, I have identified them with the names of our months. When I ran out of these, I gave the thirteenth moon, the Moon of the Moles, the expandable name December-January.

Fortunately, the animals do not need calendars, for names or no names, sun-time or moon-time, they follow their own inner clocks.

—Jean Craighead George

IN THE THIRD MOON of the year the first thaw came. Warm winds blew for days and nights. Lakes of ice turned to water. The snow slipped away. The frost let go of the soil. The Northern Hemisphere was tilting into the sun, and even the polar winds could not stop the coming of spring. The warmth penetrated the dark, rich soil in Michigan and southern Canada and thawed the last holdouts of winter: the floors of the woodlands and their ephemeral ponds. Sequestered among old hemlocks and maples, beeches and oaks, these ponds, unlike lakes and permanent ponds, are here in March, gone in August.

The first spring thaw was followed by the first spring rain. Water poured from the clouds. The cold ponds filled to their brims and set a dark stage for the ancient ritual of the mole salamanders, one of the seven families, or groups, of salamanders that live in North America, the continent where most of the salamanders dwell.

From looking at fossils, we know that one billion three hundred million years ago, limy sea plants developed in the seas. Some five hundred million years ago, shellfish and other animals without backbones evolved. They were followed by fishlike creatures that did have backbones. In another 60 million years plants appeared on the land. Sea scorpions were large and numerous, and countless kinds of shelled animals dwelled in the primitive oceans. When another 30 million years had passed, fishes were common in salt and fresh water. The first forests flourished in vast swamps.

Into this lush landscape evolved the amphibians, animals who dared to come ashore for part of their lives. They were followed by land animals, insects, reptiles, small dinosaurs, birds, big dinosaurs, as well as the flowering plants. A mere 60 million years ago, the first mammals, characterized by hair and warm blood, developed among the feet of massive horned and armored dinosaurs. The early mammals were small and awkward, but like the fish and birds, the reptiles and sea creatures, they changed and evolved. The plants also changed and evolved, as did the land and atmosphere.

But not the salamanders. Hidden in the darkness of the earth, in caves, under rocks and logs, most moving only in the blackest hours of night, they have remained unchanged for some 330 million years. The salamanders today look like the first salamanders on earth. Like those first salamanders, they still have soft legs, clawless toes, moist bodies, and eyes that do not move. The grooves along the sides of their bodies have been passed unchanged from generation to generation. They still live part of their life in water and part on land, as do the other amphibians, the frogs and toads.

The spotted salamander, a handsome member of the mole salamander family, dwells in the dark, wet soil from the Gaspé Peninsula to central Ontario and south to Georgia and Texas. Every year in the north, on the night of the first spring rain after the first spring thaw, the spotted salamanders come out of hibernation. They act out a strange and ancient drama just as they did 330 million years ago.

One of these actors awoke under the soil in a woodland in Michigan. Like all mole salamanders, he was a creature of the darkness. He lifted his

head and heard the thaw. It purled. He listened to the rain. It tapped.

He listened. He did not listen with ears on the outside of his head, for he had none, but with primitive ears that lay inside the head and along his body and tail, much like the hearing organs of the fishes. These "body ears" pick up subtle sounds in the water and the earth. He heard the tapping of the rain. It grew heavier. The spotted salamander pushed up on his short, soft legs and stepped forward. He moved slowly and awkwardly, for he was not well adapted for walking on land.

He was big, almost nine inches long, and between fifteen and twenty-five years old. Not only did he look like his early ancestors, he behaved like them. He ate insects and worms, and he lived in earthen darkness as they did. Like them he returned to the water once a year on the

night of the first spring rain after the first spring thaw. This was his night to go.

Slowly, the salamander walked to the edge of the log under which he lived. Light-yellow spots lined either side of his black body from his eyes to the tip of his tail. His belly was slate gray. He was missing a left toe, but he would not be crippled for long. Salamanders can regenerate lost feet, toes, and tails.

At the edge of his log he felt the night air. He listened to the tap of the rain. The tap became a spurtle, then a roar. Water cascaded over his log, soaked him, and gave him courage. He strode out into the night.

Half swimming, half slithering, he moved across the woodland floor. After a short distance his swishing tail touched a wood snail, coiled deep in its shell. The salamander paused. His body had heard small scratching noises inside the wood snail's shell, sounds so small only a salamander could hear them.

The scratching sound was the snail opening its winter doors. When cold weather had arrived last fall, the snail had pulled into its shell. It had rested and laid down a layer of calcium and then pulled further in. It then laid down another layer of calcium. Eventually it was sealed deep in its shell for the winter.

A few days ago the snail had felt the warming of the earth and had begun unlocking its doors with thrusts and pushes. When the salamander's tail struck, the wood snail stopped unlatching, fearful that the thump might be an enemy.

The salamander, upon hearing no more sounds from the shell, pushed on through the rain. The snail slid its foot out, then its head, unfolded its long eye stalks, and looked upon the watery shapes on the lowly landscape. To learn more about them it pushed one of its soft antennae out of its head. It felt pummeling rain, pulled back into its shell, and shut its door. It was a land snail, not a water snail.

The salamander liked the rain. Each torrent of water was transportation for him. When a rivulet washed over him, he would be picked up and carried closer to his destination. One gush of rainwater swept him over the budding fiddle-heads of a wood fern and the hump of a first bloodroot stalk. When he was finally dropped on the wet leaves, he lifted his blunt nose, took a bearing, and tramped on.

Other spotted salamanders felt the call of the moon of March. From under logs and stones, up from root-deep hideouts and buried dens, they emerged by the hundreds in the Michigan woods. A slithering parade, they moved downhill with the runoff.

From a hollow of a sugar maple tree, a screech owl saw the salamander swishing along in the parade. He was a tempting meal for the owl, but not tonight. Even a hungry screech owl would not fly in this downpour. Tree trunks were waterfalls, rock surfaces were cascades, and leaf dams created lakes. The owl retreated into his dry hollow. The salamander trod on.

The spotted salamander swung his head and tail as he moved. When he was halfway down the hill, a dam of leaves broke behind him and a deluge of water picked him up and swept him around a rock.

He paddled his feet and tail and swam. On the far side of the rock, the water spread out, soaked into the ground, and vanished. He was dumped on the forest floor. He paused to take in the sounds and tastes of the night and quickly sensed he was facing in the wrong direction. Feeling the

call of water to his right, he turned and walked downhill. Behind him came the silent parade of marching salamanders, their wet bodies shining in the rain.

Another leaf dam broke. The water rushed beside him. On it floated a struggling casebearer moth. The moth had spent the winter as a larva inside a silk-and-leaf-reinforced case he had made. When the air had grown cool last autumn, he had fastened the case to the bark of a wild cherry tree and crawled in for the winter. Just before the salamander awoke from hibernation, the young moth emerged from his case. He fought his way out and rested. His wings unfolded. His feet hardened. His antennae feathered out. He was ready to fly when the rain struck. Water rolled down the tree trunk and washed him into the woods, where he crawled onto a dam made of leaves. He was preparing to fly when it broke.

He went rushing past the salamander. Although he was salamander food, the long, chunky amphibian ignored him and strode on.

The salamander's four-toed front foot pushed back a leaf and uncovered the tip of a spring beauty. This forest flower raced to bloom before the tree leaves emerged and cast it in shade. Other spring flowers were hurrying to bloom. Two of them were the marsh marigolds in the wooded wetlands and the hepatica of the hillsides. The hepatica, a shiny-leafed plant, had not died in the winter. It had just stopped growing. When the warmth returned, it proceeded to grow again as if winter had never happened.

The salamander pushed against a hepatica leaf and thumped on. He did not see the plant, for salamander eyes see only things that move. They cannot see still objects.

The eyes of the salamander do not rotate, like

the eyes of the mammals and birds, an attribute that helps creatures to see inanimate objects. To a salamander, if a moth does not move, a worm wiggle, or a leaf twist, then the world is a blank piece of paper. With the water moving an acorn along, the salamander saw it. Not only did he see the nut, but a worm on the nut. The worm was the larva of an acorn borer. It had wiggled out of the acorn when the flood struck and was now riding the rapids to somewhere.

Although the salamander would have snapped up the worm at any other time, he was not interested now. He had come to the edge of the woodland pond. It was the same pond to which he and his ancestors had come every year on the night of the first rain after the first spring thaw. The pond was a transient ecosystem. It dried up in summer.

The shallow pond water was black with tannin from the leaves. Because the pond dried up in

summer, no fish could live in it. Without these predators to devour them, many delicate and remarkable creatures, including the salamanders, could live out their water lives in safety here.

The pond had a voice. It was the weeping of rain on water. The salamander remembered the voice and walked toward it. Suddenly he was swimming. He was a water creature again.

Small animals swirled around him, but they were too small for the salamander to see. They had awakened from winter's hibernation and were traveling about the pond. Some whipped past him flapping hairlike cilia. Others floated and wiggled their one-celled bodies. The pond teemed with life, but unlike the permanent ponds that held many different species, the transient ponds harbored only a few varieties—microscopic life, little crustaceans, a few changeling insects, and the amphibians. Transient ponds held few species, but many of each.

A black canoe-shaped whirligig beetle popped up from his hibernation place in the mud and rested on the surface. He sat very still looking in two directions with his four eyes. Two eyes looked up into the air, two looked down into the water. The beetle's ability to see in both the water and the air, as well as up and down, was the perfect solution for a creature that lives on the surface of the water where enemies and food come from both above and below.

Passing the spinning whirligig, the salamander looked at him and swam on. The movements of his legs and his body, so clumsy on land, were now as graceful as circling smoke. He turned his head and spiraled to the bottom of the pond.

Other salamanders had joined him. They rolled, circled, and arched as they began the ancient spring dance of the spotted salamanders.

The salamander dived over a floating oak leaf and swam down among a gathering of fairy shrimp. These beautiful red-and-blue crustaceans are distant relatives of the lobsters and crayfish. They are creatures of the spring, existing only in the transient ponds where fish cannot eat them. Seeing the salamander, they darted away on their backs, their hearts and stomachs visible through their glittering, transparent bodies. One hid behind a stick. Her black eyes, large for her tiny body, shone brightly on their little stalks. The tiny creature was on her back, for fairy shrimp live and travel feet up. She waved her "leaf-feet" gills, through which she breathed. She also used them to swim. The leaf-feet also operate like fingers and teeth. They pick up one-celled animals and plants, chew them with the gnawing tips and put them in the tiny mouth.

The salamander came up under the fairy

shrimp, saw her slender heart beating in her glassy body, and swam on.

He was not interested in the fairy shrimp, or the hundreds of other little female fairy shrimp who were carrying their eggs in pockets on their bellies. In the salamander's pond there were only a few male fairy shrimp and sometimes none at all. Consequently, most of the eggs the female carried were not fertilized. Yet they would develop and grow in the mysterious way of nature called parthenogenesis. Under the moons of April and May, the fairy shrimp eggs, fertilized and unfertilized, would fall from the brood pockets of the females and sink to the bottom of the pond. When August dried up the pond, they would become "resting eggs," eggs that estivate, the summer equivalent of hibernate, through the heat and drought. When the water returned in the spring they would hatch into fairy shrimp larvae and mature with the thaw. The crystalline adults would swim with the salamanders, the one-celled animals and plants, and the whirligigs, in a celebration of the return of the transient pond.

The salamander danced on. He passed close to the pond's edge. A spring peeper, the tiniest frog in the forest, sat upon a stick. The peeper did not move. He had just awakened, and he was still too cold to hop. He was waiting for the earth to warm several more degrees; then he would leap along the pond edge and sing the first spring song of the frogs.

In the mud and leaves below the peeper sat the next frog to come out of hibernation, the wood frog. He was huddled down in the cold leaves, also silent and still. He needed more heat than the peeper to start him singing.

The salamander swam out from the shore.

A female came toward him. They met. For a moment they drifted with their forearms and legs outspread; then the male circled her, twisting and rolling. The female swam upward in graceful loops. Another female joined the dancers. Two more males crossed the pond and slowly circled the females.

For hours and hours they danced. As the moon passed its apogee behind a barricade of rain clouds, the ancient ballet approached the finale. The salamanders dived, spiraled, and drifted faster and faster. The yellow spots on their sides shone like lanterns in the water. The lanterns glowed at all levels—the bottom, the middle, and the surface.

Then the spotted salamander dove under his female, lifted her on his nose, and carried her into deep water. He clasped her with his front legs, then released her.

She drifted. He descended to the bottom of the pond and laid a small white object on a leaf. The object looked like a collar button. It was a spermatophore, the tip of which held the DNA code of the male spotted salamander, the magic that would start the growth of the next generation.

The button laid, the spotted salamander swam away. Slowly, quietly, the female drifted down upon it, and the spermatozoa entered her body. The button remained on the leafy bottom.

The dance was done. The spotted salamander climbed ashore; the female surfaced, paddled to a leafy beach, and began walking back to her home.

The sky lightened above the Michigan woods. In the transient pond, white spermatophores grew dull, one-celled animals whipped their cilia, fairy shrimp swam on their backs, and whirligigs looked up and down. But there was not a salamander to be seen.

When the sun arose, the spotted salamander was in darkness under his log.

A sharp tap on the tree above him announced the arrival of morning. The downy woodpecker was chipping a nest hole. He did not work long. Nest building was just beginning, and like most beginnings in nature, it was slow. The woodpecker heard another woodpecker tapping. He flew off to see who it was. Neighbors were more important to the bird at this time of year than nest building. He was setting up boundaries around his home and must check to make sure there were no trespassers.

The spotted salamander lay still in his dark world.

Just after daylight, the winds shook the trees, which trembled their roots and the earth around them. The salamander listened. The weather was changing. Cold air from the north had met the warm air above the thawed land, and the clash brewed turbulent gusts. The freeze would return. Snows would fall. The winter weather in Michigan had not come to an end.

The next night before the temperature dropped, the female salamander left her shelter under a stone and took the long road to the pond. Other females returned with her, and once more the spring pond became a stage for the salamanders.

The female circled and pirouetted until she found a firm twig toward the middle of the pond where the water would not dry up too soon. She put her soft front legs around it. She pressed the five toes of her back feet against it. From her body spilled a mass of glittering black eggs.

At first the eggs were dots, round and tightly packed together. A thin layer of gelatinous

material surrounded each egg. The material swelled when the eggs struck the water and formed a protective cover.

Her eggs clung to the stick just under the surface of the water. The female swam back to land and walked to her retreat. The transient pond would be mother to her offspring. It would keep them cool and moist. It would buoy the slender four-legged larvae that would hatch in May or June depending on the temperature of the water. It would give air to the gills that would stand up like ruffs behind their heads, and it would support the one-celled life and the microscopic crustaceans that the salamander larvae would eat. They would grow and thrive.

In August the salamander larvae, the fairy shrimp, and the other changelings would be ready for the drought. Just as the water was about to vanish, the gills of the salamanders would disappear, and the adult salamanders would have air-breathing lungs. The timing of the shift from water breathers to air breathers would be perfect. As little adults they would leave the pond and burrow into the moist leaves and soil to live underground like their parents.

The fairy shrimp would also be prepared for the drastic change—the adults would have died, but not their resting eggs. The insects would simply metamorphose and fly away. The one-celled plants and animals would survive in the mud. The transient pond would be asleep for the summer.

As the March moon waned, the salamander heard spring noises in the soil around him. Beetle larvae were chewing roots; centipedes and sow bugs were hustling food. A chipmunk was digging a nursery in the ground far down below him. Getting to his feet, the salamander took a secret

trail from his retreat to the underside of a stone. An earthworm wiggled. The salamander saw the worm, snapped it up, and ate.

The moon of the salamanders was done.

Bibliography

Billings, Charlene W. *Salamanders*. New York: Dodd, Mead, 1981.

———. *Salamanders As Pets*. New York: Dodd, Mead, 1981.

Bishop, Sherman C. *Handbook of Salamanders*. New York: Hafner Publishing Company, 1962.

Cochran, Doris M. *Living Amphibians of the World*. Garden City, NY: Doubleday & Company, 1961.

Compton's Encyclopedia. Vol. 22, p. 25. Chicago: Encyclopedia Britannica Inc., 1980.

Conant, Roger. *A Field Guide to Reptiles and Amphibians of Eastern and Central North America*. Boston: Houghton Mifflin Company, 1975.

Morgan, Ann Haven. *Field Book of Ponds and Streams*. New York: G.P. Putnam's Sons, 1930.

The World Book Encyclopedia. Vol. 17, p. 53. Chicago: World Book Inc., 1983.

Index